APPLICATION PERFORMANCE MANAGEMENT

A Practical Introduction

DR SAMPATH PRAKASH
JOHN SIKORA

ISBN: 0615598897
ISBN 13: 9780615598895

Sampath Prakash: To My Loving Mother

CONTENTS

Praise for Application Performance Management

"I am personally very familiar with the authors of this fantastic book. I can speak directly to their high level of professionalism and expertise. As it relates to the book itself I found it to be very useful and practical as it relates to need to analyze and understand how application performance management can and will have a direct impact on the overall performance of enterprise networks. I highly recommend this to any technology leader who is interesting in improving their business."

-Tom Clement, SVP, Edgenet

◦◦◦

"Most applications and services are built and sold today as packages, with modules built with a focus on functionality and ease of integration. While this shortens the time to market, performance (and security) of the finished product and service is compromised, and not caught during the QA and testing phases. The problems surface in the production environment often over the wide area networks. By that time, remediation becomes both intrusive and expensive.

This book is a compilation of techniques and approaches to address the performance aspects of applications and services proactively as well as post-implementation. The experience the authors of this book have gained across a wide spectrum of corporations in various sectors is condensed for an aspiring practitioner as well as a decision-maker."

SUNIL NADKARNI, DIRECTOR, GLOBAL WIDE AREA NETWORK OPERATIONS, McGRAW-HILL

"In my job, we conduct migration of data centers involving Mainframe and Open System Servers for large global companies. Network connectivity and its performance are the key elements of any successful migration. This book "Application Performance Management" gives an insight how to improve the performance through a detailed technical description which can be understood easily by managers like me. I highly recommend this book to not only to my NW staff but also clients who usually own the application during migrations."

- BASAVARAJ, SENIOR GLOBAL IT DELIVERY MANAGER FOR A WELL KNOWN SW/HW/SERVICES COMPANY

"This book is an excellent compilation of the causes of application performance problems and solutions in an easily-understandable format. This is perhaps one of the best overview books for a beginner or a specialist. Great job!"

-JOHN, SENIOR VP OF A MAJOR TELECOM SERVICES COMPANY

PREFACE

In the last forty years, we have evolved from wired terminal-to-mainframe applications to mobile Apps on smart phones/tablets. The underlying network has evolved from speeds of a few kilobits per sec to tens or even hundreds of megabits per sec. What has not changed is the frequent frustration of users stuck with slow response times. The battle for improving performance is as perpetual as the evolution of technology itself.

This book is based mostly on our real life, decade-long consulting experience with clients, supplemented with industry research. The authors currently work at Apsera Tech Inc., and prior to that they had a long tenure at AT&T Corp.

We have focused on making the reader understand Application Performance Management (APM) topics, issues, and solutions at a conceptual level but tied to real-life scenarios and implementations. As a result, the book can be useful to multiple audiences: business application owners, performance engineers, managers, project managers, application developers, user experience specialists, testers, and senior level under-graduate and graduate students.

The APM discipline has existed for decades through its manifestation in its component fields such as server performance and network performance. It is only in the last few years that APM became a unified discipline and gained traction, mainly because the end-user has become a "customer" in the huge and fast-growing e-commerce industry.

APM issues span across multiple disciplines such as software, networking, server engineering, and user interface engineering. Since these disciplines typically operate in silos, APM issues can always be expected to arise. It is our sincere hope that this book will increase awareness of APM issues and techniques among all concerned and help bridge these silos of expertise.

ACKNOWLEDGEMENTS

I t is such a pleasure to be writing this note of *Acknowledgements* on Thanksgiving Day of 2011 while approaching the completion of this book. Our first exposure to the field of APM happened in the year 2000 when the authors and their AT&T team were helping JP Morgan Chase with their application performance issues. The work later lead into a professional service offering that was called WAN Application Readiness Testing (WANart). We have, since then, been helping many corporations, big and small, with their APM issues through our company Apsera Tech Inc.

We fondly recall and would like to thank all the members of our WANart team. Some names certainly stand out in our minds – Tarun Kapoor, Sunil Nadkarni, Uday Puro, Anto Joseph, Sumit Sahay, Kwasi Yeboah-Afihene, Ted Flamoropoulos, Nik Chinai, Jeff Jaggernauth, Mario Figueroa, Ling-Ling Li, Iona Patrascu, Sampath Rengarajan, Les Correia, and Manshi Joisher. We would like to thank the AT&T Network Integration management (Jin-shi Chen, in particular) and engagement managers for giving us the opportunity to work with various AT&T clients. Special thanks to Angela Esposito for her consistent help and support.

A big thanks to OPNET Technologies and their engineers – it is an understatement to say that we learned many APM concepts from them. OPNET tools have been indispensable in our APM work.

We would like to thank Durga Kotikalapudi for patiently going through the manuscript and helping with the editing. Special thanks belong to Pooja Kini, Amrutha Kini, and Shekar Avadhani for the final round of patient editing.

We bring out this book with great humility, recognizing that the field of APM is full of innovators with great contributions. Our wish is simply to help promote awareness of this exciting field among managers, practitioners, and students, and help the field grow further.

CHAPTER 1

"Not everything that counts can be counted, and not everything that can be counted counts."

-ALBERT EINSTEIN

WHY WORRY ABOUT APPLICATION PERFORMANCE?

When you walk into a dark room and flip a switch, the room is lighted instantaneously. That is what users expect when they click (or touch, these days) on an application tab on the computer screen – instant response. The human brain is wired to expect response times under 1-2 seconds when any interactive activity such as browsing on the web is performed.

The consequences of slow response times are more than just a minor inconvenience or annoyance to the user. If you are an e-commerce website, your users often hop to another site when they don't get responses in a few seconds, causing loss of potential revenue. If your employees' business applications like SAP or Oracle are slow, there is loss of productivity. If the prescription application at a pharmacy check out is slow, you can have long lines resulting in poor customer satisfaction.

If you are a trader in New York Stock Exchange, you would expect your trades to be completed in sub-second times – millions of dollars could be at stake on a volatile day.

The single most important metric of application (App, as popularly called) performance is the *response time* as perceived by a user while executing an application transaction or a sub-task. *Response time* is the elapsed time in seconds when a user clicks on a button and receives the full response he or she is expecting. Note that response time is also your "wait time" (while you are staring at the hourglass or rotating circle on the screen) for your task to complete.

Sometimes aggregate measures such as throughput or download speeds are used in the context of application performance. For example, your friend may say that she is getting a 10 Mbits/sec download speed on her new iPhone. Although the higher this number is, the better it is (as you will see later in the book) it does not necessarily mean you are getting a fast response time for your application.

Good application performance is just one component, but an important one, of user experience. Factors such as ease of use, ease of navigation, page aesthetics, and multi-media enhancements also contribute to a great user experience. Another interesting aspect to note is that a user may expend quite a bit of time doing what is known as "think time" – viewing/reading the screen, figuring out or finding what to input, inputting the data, or even multi-tasking on another application. But when one is ready and clicks a button, one *expects* an instantaneous response.

Application Performance Management (APM) as intended in this work is the science and art of defining, engineering, measuring, analyzing, improving, trouble-shooting, and controlling response times of multiple applications for the end-users (who could number in hundreds of millions if you are running Google or Facebook).

Another closely related terminology in this field is Application Performance ***Monitoring*** which focuses on the on-going operational aspects of Application Performance once an Application is deployed in the field ; we would use ***Management*** as a broader term here in this book that includes monitoring.

CHAPTER 2

WHY IS MY APPLICATION SLOW?

WHAT IS IN THE PATH?

Before we delve into why an application is slow, we need to understand the components and physical /logical paths involved in the execution of an application transaction. Let us look at the Figure below, a diagrammatic example simplified for easy understanding.

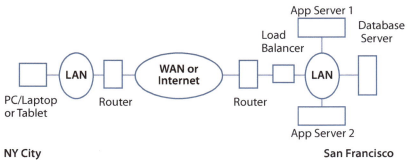

Figure 1 A Typical Networked Application Path

An end-user, say in New York City, who may be using a desktop PC, laptop, tablet or a smart phone is connected to a local area network. The application path starts through this local network shown generically as "LAN" which could be a wired or a wireless LAN, or a mobile network (3G or 4G) from a telecom company. The application path then goes through a router to a company WAN (Wide Area Network) or Internet provided by an ISP such as Comcast or AT&T.

The application path goes further through the far-end router in a data center, and then the load balancer connects to either one of the App servers. The path continues from the App server to the Database server as needed. The load balancers, App servers, and Database server(s) are on a high speed LAN in the data center, say in San Francisco.

An application transaction has to pass through network devices (switches, routers, and load balancers), physical network links (copper or fiber), wireless links, and servers. In many real life scenarios there are not only a multiplicity of these types of components but other types of components not shown, such as a firewall or a proxy server.

The bits belonging to packets of the application transaction have to travel a distance of 2563 miles from New York to San Francisco at a speed somewhat less than the speed of light in vacuum (taking into account the refractive index of the glass fiber, this speed is about 124,188 mps rather than 186,282 mps) – this journey takes about 21 milliseconds (one way). Actually, it is greater as the path is often not a straight line between the two cities. This transit delay is known as *latency*, and although it looks like a very small number, we will later see how it can still have a large effect on performance.

The different links in the transaction path can carry information "bits" at different speeds, and this rate of transmission is known as **bandwidth**. In a LAN, the bandwidth can range from tens of megabits per second to several gigabits per second. In a slow link somewhere on the WAN (typically at the edges), the bandwidth may be only a few hundred kilobits/sec (let us hope we never have to go back to the dial-up days where we were getting just tens of kilobits per sec!).

Note that the word "speed" is used in two different ways when referring to latency and bandwidth. In a highway analogy where a car acts as "one bit," the latency would be the time it takes for one car to travel (at the speed limit) from one city to another, whereas the bandwidth or "bit speed" would be analogous to the number of cars that can pass a given point on a highway between the cities in a given unit of time (which is more dependent on the width of the highway and/or the size of the cars). Thus, bandwidth or bit speed is actually a measure of link capacity.

Bandwidth and Latency are thus two different but very important factors contributing to slow response times. In a LAN, one can assume very large bandwidth (let us exaggerate it to infinity) and negligible latency (let us play it down to zero). If your PC and the application server happen to be on the same LAN (possible, for example, when you are working in the corporate headquarters where the data center is also located) and your server is very lightly loaded, your application response time for a normally functioning application should be sub-second.

However, in this age of Internet and networked computing, your PC and the application server are most likely to be across a WAN. In addition to latency and bandwidth, a host of other factors will come into play and you will be very unlikely to get the LAN-like sub-second response time that you may desire.

WHAT ARE THE DIFFERENT COMPONENTS OF THE RESPONSE TIME?

So far, we have a pretty good idea of what the different devices involved in a typical application transaction path are. Now let us see how these devices interact and what other aspects come into play causing transaction wait time for the user.

The pie chart below (Figure 2) shows a sample transaction of a Business Objects application which was very slow for the customer. This particular transaction was captured by a sniffer as it was being executed by a user and analyzed using a tool from OPNET. The transaction itself took 298 seconds or almost 5 minutes.

Server-side Processing (highlighted in yellow in the Figure 2) The highest component of the response time (about 170 seconds) is the application processing time on the server side. This component would include processing by the application server and the database server. A further drilldown (using OPNET, for example) would reveal where exactly the delay came from. Examples of server delay are server capacity or memory constraints, inefficient logic in the application, and slow database queries.

Client-side Processing (highlighted in yellow in the Figure 2) Note that there is also a processing delay, although much smaller, at the client side. This is the processing time (15 seconds) the client machine (in this case a PC) is taking, to perform tasks on its side and display results. The Client here could also be a laptop, smartphone, or even another server acting as a client of the server at the other end.

Network Bandwidth (highlighted in green in the Figure 2) The next significant component of the response time (91 seconds), after the server, is the one attributable to the limited bandwidth in the network path. In this case the WAN bandwidth was 2 Mbits/sec and the amount of data bytes that had to be transferred from the server to the client was 23.2 Mbytes.

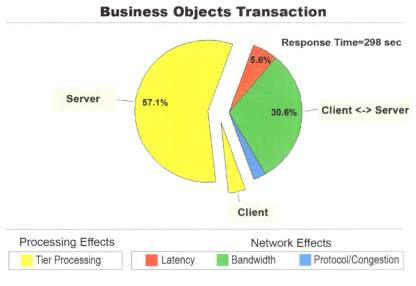

Figure 2 Response Time Components

Network Latency (highlighted red in the Figure 2) The next component of the response time (about 17 seconds) is due to the latency of the WAN between the client and the server. This delay is a direct result of the chattiness of the application. The client is asking the server for small pieces of information at a time and the server returns the requested information. In this particular case, there are 690 times during which the client is requesting small pieces of information. This repeated exchange of information over a WAN link could cost considerable time as each request-response exchange takes one round-trip delay (or twice the one-way latency) to complete. The one-way latency between the server and the client is by itself only 50 to 100 milliseconds, but because of excessive number of request-response exchanges, the total time attributable to latency has added up to 17 seconds.

One-way latency is generally never more than 100 – 200 milliseconds but the amplification effect of chattiness of the application can make the delay due to latency a major component of response time. Historically, many older applications were designed to run on a LAN with latency close to zero, so chattiness was ignored, and many companies have simply ported those applications to run over a WAN, resulting in slow response times.

Although there is no standard measurement for application chattiness, a term that is frequently used is "application turns", which denotes the number of times the application information flow changes direction. Sometimes, a number which is one-half of "application turns" and represents the number of client-server exchanges is also quoted. The best way is to refer to the definition the particular tool vendor is using.

Protocol (part of blue slice in the Figure 2) Most interactive applications use the ***Transmission Control Protocol (TCP)*** which is the language of communication between the client and the server to transfer data back and forth. TCP is a robust protocol that guarantees that all the bytes of information that are transmitted are received error free and in the sequence that they were sent. TCP segments are carried over hop by hop across routers in the Internet or a company WAN by the ***Internet Protocol (IP)***.

IP works like a good faith post-office service and delivers packets based on best effort (known as datagram service) – occasionally the packets could be lost or get corrupted. The TCP which runs across end-to-end corrects such deficiencies.

TCP was designed in the 1970's when network speeds were slow and the error rates in the transmission facilities were somewhat high. It is also a conservative protocol that is sensitive to not worsening an existing congestion condition in the network by pumping more packets, and hence will tend to slow down when it detects congestion. Today's WAN and Internet facilities are mainly comprised of high speed and almost error-free fiber optic links, and TCP often does not exploit these characteristics, especially when its parameters are set to expect older networking technology.

The noticeable *response time* component belonging to TCP protocol is a result of un-optimized parameters such as TCP window size and other parameters pertaining to the protocol mechanism.

Congestion (part of blue slice in Figure 2) occurs when an outgoing transmission link on a router is running at or near its maximum capacity, and the incoming packets are queued up in a buffer and have to wait their turn. The cumulative delay because of queuing is identified in the "congestion" bucket of the response time.

Packets may also sometimes be dropped before getting into the queue because of lack of buffer space that might be caused by excessive congestion. Such packets are retransmitted by the TCP protocol. Packets that are dropped because of errors are also retransmitted by TCP. Since the effects of congestion are corrected by the protocol it might make sense to put the response time components of protocol and congestion in the same bucket.

The above classification of delays, although somewhat at a high level, is very helpful for understanding end-user response time and can be used for both developing preventive strategies and conducting trouble-shooting exercises. One simplification we have made here is to assume that the delay components are occurring in some sequence and there is no overlap in the delays. In practice, some combination of delays could occur in parallel and does help in reducing the overall response time.

CHAPTER 3

HOW DO I PREVENT APPLICATION SLOWNESS?

STAKEHOLDERS IN THE GAME

The end-user is clearly the most important, but not always the most powerful stakeholder – it is no fun being forced to use a slow application. But if you are an end-user stuck with a slow performing application, it is not clear whether you are always going to get help. It depends heavily on what "role" you are playing in being an end-user. Obviously not all users are created equal. If you are visiting an informational website with few advertisements and if it is slow, you are unlikely to get help. On the other hand if you are accessing an informational website that depends on the advertisements for revenue, you are likely get help sooner or later. For example, the fact that Google search takes into account page download times in determining its rankings is a big help.

If you are a knowledge worker in a big company and if your applications are slow, you may not get immediate help. Persistent complaining to the help desk eventually makes the IT department spend the time necessary to fix the problem. Corporations have gained awareness of the App performance issues in the last few years and are more willing to deploy solutions such as WAN Optimization that provide great relief.

If you are a clerk working in the Accounts Payable department of a large company, and the application you use to process enquiries from suppliers for their invoices is slow, help may not come that quickly. But if you are a call center worker pulling customer data while answering calls and your application is slow, you are very likely to receive prompt help. The reason is that a slow application affects customer satisfaction and drives the operating costs of the call center higher, as the agents spend more time with the customer to answer queries.

In a medium or large enterprise when an application is reported as performing poorly, the Network Managers are typically the scapegoats – they are deemed guilty unless proven otherwise. The Network Managers typically would have installed a multiplicity of network performance tools that show that the WAN links are not over-utilized, the latencies and packet losses are minimal, the switches/routers are not overloaded, and there are no routing or queuing issues. Sometimes they have to produce pie charts like the one in Figure 2 you saw earlier to prove to the application owners that the network is not at fault for poor performance.

Application Owners from the business unit side as well as their counterparts on the IT side have the most at stake in ensuring that their application meets or exceeds the end-users' performance expectations. Application owners are involved in the life-cycle of the application, and set the right direction for planning, development, testing, deployment, and ongoing monitoring of their application. They have the budget to implement best practices, processes, hardware, software, and tools to ensure their application performs well and meets the business objectives.

Since there are hundreds of business critical applications in a company and many application owners, it makes organizational sense to have a Chief Performance Officer (CPO) akin to a Chief Security Officer (CSO). The CPO can help in sharing the best practices, processes, and tools needed to achieve superior application performance among multiple application owners across different business units.

The last but not the least important stakeholder in application performance is again the end-user, but this time the user has her credit card next to her mouse. If an e-commerce site takes more than 5 seconds, the user may not even continue shopping at that site. The user may abandon a loaded cart if it takes 7 seconds or more to check out. Now, there is a lot more at stake for the e-commerce company to ensure that users get very fast response times – this is good news for the whole APM industry.

TYPICAL SCENARIO FOR A NEW APPLICATION

Let us take the example of a nationwide bank wanting to provide PC banking services to its customers via the Internet. We will call it the 'e-Banking' application (e-Banking App). Mary is the product manager for this application and also the business owner. A business case has been made that indicated there is a good Return-on-investment (ROI) if 80% of the customers use the e-Banking application, cutting down most routine visits to the branches, and also increasing customer satisfaction. The IT department has estimated that it takes a year to plan, develop, test, and roll-out e-Banking to all the customers. Steve, one of the VPs in the IT department, is in charge of the delivery of the 'e-Banking' application. The new application will be accessed from a customer's browser via the bank's website which is currently only informational.

The development team has completed the coding of the application and various functional tests have been done to ascertain the application works as intended. Steve is aware that he needs servers that can handle 1000 customer sessions simultaneously and he makes sure proper server load testing is done in the lab to size the servers (both the App server and the database server). Server load testing has become an integral part of the Software Development Life-cycle (SDLC) for the last 15 years or so and it usually is not a neglected step even with mid-sized companies.

If Steve deploys the 'e-Banking application' at this stage, it is very likely that many customers will complain that the application is slow. Many of them may stop using the application and continue their visits to the bank. The promised ROI may not be realized and it is doubtful that Mary is considered a hero in the eyes of her VP.

On the other hand, if Steve has some exposure to the APM industry and he is aware of the potentially devastating effects of the Internet/WAN on an application, he would add a couple of steps to his testing methodology. Even prior to that, he would have discussed with Mary the acceptable level of *response times* for each of the customer transactions. Mary may even demand a Service Level Agreement (SLA) for the most common if not all customer transactions, in the e-Banking App. At a minimum level Mary may demand that no transaction exceeds, say, 5 seconds in *response time*.

Best Practices for APM Pre-deployment Testing

The lack of awareness, or insufficient planning time, or casual attitude among developers and testers towards visualizing and understanding how a new application is eventually deployed in the field, are the primary causes of application performance issues. Many times, because of silo mentality and inefficient flow of information, the developers/testers may not be briefed properly on the environment (global WAN or Internet) over which the App is routinely going to be used. Fortunately this situation is changing slowly for the better.

Coming back to the 'e-Banking App', once the functional testing is completed and the application logic is working as it is intended, testing needs to be done to ascertain how the App will perform over the WAN.

There are two type of tools – simulation based and emulation based – to help in this regard. The emulation type of tool is appliance based with configurable quantities for typical WAN parameters – bandwidth, latency, packet loss, and jitter (if voice or video is involved). A single-user testing can be easily incorporated in the testing stage of the SDLC.

In the case of our e-Banking App, since it is going to be used over the Internet, a range of values needs to be assumed for bandwidth, latency, and packet loss for setting up in the emulator tool. The emulation tool, mimicking the characteristics of internet transmission, sits between a single-user and the App server in the lab. The *response time* can thus be tested for each of the possible App transactions over the WAN (in this case, Internet). The previous testing attempt which caused performance problems was carried out over a LAN in the lab and was oblivious to the presence of the WAN.

If it is prohibitive to test all transactions, at least the most frequently used App transactions (e.g., login, check balance, pay bill) need to be tested. If the *response time* does not meet the agreed upon objectives (in this case 5 seconds), the root cause has to be identified and the App has to go back to the developers for remediation. It is a lot cheaper to fix the App at this point of the Software Development Life-Cycle than after it is deployed in the field.

Once the App yields acceptable transaction response times for a single user, it can be passed on to the next stage – multi-user load testing [1]. Even at this stage it is strongly recommended that the load testing be carried out over the same emulated WAN. When App *response times* are larger, the server needs to hold the resources (processing power and memory) longer for TCP-level processing. Presenting a realistic type of load to the server over the emulated WAN ensures that the server is designed to reflect real-life conditions.

It is possible that some *response time* issues are discovered during load testing. There may be issues in the application at the software component level (JAVA or .Net). Sophisticated tools are available in the market place to identify these types of issues.

Instead of WAN emulation tools, simulation tools that model WAN characteristics can also be used. To use a simulation tool, various user transactions have to be captured (with a packet Sniffer or Wireshark or similar software) as they are executed by a user. These captures, when imported into the simulation tool, can reveal important characteristics of the App transactions such as amount of data bytes transferred and chattiness, which can be red flags. The tool will also be able to predict the App *response times* of those transactions under study in a real WAN environment (in this case the Internet). If the prediction does not produce the desired App *response times*, the application has to be modified and fine tuned until the objectives are met.

Unlike the WAN emulation tools, simulation tools usually come with associated software components (agents) that reside on the servers and/or the PCs to collect the data needed for input into the simulation. The simulation tools can provide detailed visibility into the end-to-end application flow that will be greatly beneficial to the App developer for modifying the code. The tools provide many what-if-scenarios that a developer can play with by tweaking parameters such as chattiness and payload.

The simulation tools can also help predict the bandwidths needed at the data center or a branch with multiple bank employees using the e-Banking application concurrently. Sizing the bandwidth and communicating this information to the network manager, will ensure enough network capacity is made available when the App is deployed to geographically dispersed locations.

The choice of type of tools may be more due to tester preference, but the most important thing is to use some decent tools in the application development/testing phase to assess the performance of the App in the actual WAN-based production environment and fix the App before it goes for field deployment.

BEST PRACTICES FOR APM IN DESIGNING WEBSITES/WEB APPLICATIONS

From the APM point of view, applications can be classified into Web/browser-based Apps and the general Client-Server Apps. Web-based applications (we will simply call them Web Apps) are launched by a user using one of the popular browsers such as Microsoft's IE, Mozilla Firefox, Google's Chrome, or Apple's

Safari. An example of a popular Client-Server application is Microsoft Outlook/Exchange. Because of the ubiquity of the Internet and the availability of industry standards (e.g., HTML) the browsers are based upon, the most common Apps today are Web-based.

One of the most frequent activities among Internet users is browsing informational sites. From a *response time* point of view the action involves the user clicking on a URL and having the web page fetched and displayed. The *response time* in this context is also referred to as page load time. Of course the users want the web pages loaded on their screens in a second or two. At some point the user may go further and invoke a transactional web application starting with a login (for web mail, shopping, bank balance viewing, etc.). This part of the application will involve more application servers and backend database servers.

From a *response time* point of view, the web pages have to download fast during the browsing part. When a user executes a web transaction, the results (e.g., bank balance, shopping confirmation, etc.) have to be delivered almost instantaneously to the user. It is observed that the front-end portion (downloading the web page) can take a significant part of the response time, if designed improperly. Hence it is very important that websites, whether they are informational or transactional or both, be designed for fast page load times. We will see below how a browser and a web server can work in concert to optimize various flows and produce fast page load times.

Websites are built with multiple purposes in mind – rendering rich visual experience, ease of navigation, e-commerce functionalities, ease of ongoing maintenance for keeping pages up to date, and various other factors. Fast page load times or end-user response times are surely a critical requirement for the user, but perhaps only on the wish list of a casual website designer/developer – the unknown and varying network characteristics of the Internet sitting between the user and the websites being the big challenge. The fact that websites are increasingly accessed by browsers on mobile devices such as smart phones and tablets with limited processing power and constrained bandwidth, makes fulfilling the fast-response time requirement harder and harder.

WAN Optimization techniques which are hugely successful in corporate environments cannot be directly imported to the web browsing case, because the classical data center-to-remote site topology does not apply to a single user visiting multiple websites. These classical techniques require matching optimization devices on each end of the communication, and a user, even if in possession of an optimization device, usually would not be able to find a matching device at the wide variety of websites.

Big Internet portals such as Google and Yahoo follow the best practices and build performance requirements right at the planning stages. They use sophisticated tools that help in making web Apps faster for their end-users. One such handy tool is **YSlow** from Yahoo. **YSlow** is a free tool that can be installed as an add-on to a Firefox browser (enabled with Firebug). It is intended for use by the website developers to help manage response time requirements. When you visit any website with the Firefox browser, **YSlow** measures the page download time and grades the website page in 23 or so categories along with some good recommendations.

Some examples of recommendations include: making fewer http requests, using Content Delivery Networks (CDNs), positioning style sheets and Java scripts, reducing DNS look-ups, and compressing and minifying techniques. **Yslow** also depicts the component weights in Kbytes for both empty cache (first time visits) and primed cache (subsequent visits). Smaller weights signify faster page load times.

Following the recommendations provided by **YSlow** in designing websites can help cut down the response time by 25% or more. **YSlow** was developed by Steve Souders when he was the performance chief at Yahoo. He is now with Google (and incidentally Google has a similar tool called Page Speed that works with the Chrome browser). Steve has also published two books [2, 3] on best practices in high performance website design which are great handbooks for any serious website designer/developer. Following the best practices detailed in the books can optimize the web pages even before they are ready for testing with **Yslow**.

One caution to note is that **Yslow** is not network "aware". Hence the website developer/tester has to create the realistic network environment (either Internet or a company WAN) by emulation techniques or by using an actual network to perform testing and fine-tune each webpage. **Yslow,** at the time of this writing, is available only for Firefox browsers and not for the more popular Internet Explorer (IE).

With the proliferation of smart phones and constant user complaints about slow access to their favorite websites, companies are scrambling to "mobilize" their websites. **YSlow** is definitely a handy tool complementing sophisticated tools, in following best practices for pre-deployment of web applications.

BEFORE A DATA CENTER RELOCATION

Large corporations typically have many data centers spread over the country or even across the continents. These data centers may have been created along with new internal business units or might correspond to business functions such as manufacturing, design, R&D, or Corporate Headquarters. Data centers are very expensive to maintain – there are costs related to power/ air conditioning, real estate, maintenance of servers, and IT personnel. There has been a trend in the last decade to consolidate data centers into one or two per global region (e.g., Americas, Asia/Pacific) to realize substantial cost savings.

Data center relocation projects are complex and expensive, and a large one could take a couple of years to complete. Typically, users access most of their applications in their local data center which is in the same building or campus. Because of the nature of the high speed LAN they use to connect with the servers, *response times* are generally good. When the data centers from various locations across the nation are consolidated into one location, often at an outsourced site, the users' application servers are no longer a LAN away – they have to traverse the WAN with varying latencies and constrained bandwidth. Many companies do not engage in the due diligence for assessing the impact of the move on end-user *response times*. Imagine a company spending two years and millions of dollars to complete the data center relocation and then discovering that users are getting unacceptable response times and it is affecting productivity (some applications simply may not run).

Luckily there are many APM-aware companies that incorporate the *response time* impact study as one of the key project tasks, right at the planning stage. The approach for the *response time* impact study is fairly straightforward. The first step is to identify the mission critical or business critical apps that users are currently accessing over the LAN in those data centers. For each of the identified applications, it will be necessary to identify the most frequently used App transactions, which typically could be five to ten in number but sometimes more. A criterion for acceptable *response times* has to be defined (for example, one could require that *response time* should not double - compared to the LAN case) - or exceed seven seconds after the move.

The second step is to decide on the use of appropriate tools to predict the performance impact – simulation based or emulation based. User participation will be necessary to baseline the current LAN performance, and then one must run WAN impact predictions with the tool. Knowing the WAN characteristics (e.g., bandwidth, latency, current traffic load, and packet loss), the tools will be able to predict the user *response times* in the scenario of a consolidated data center. Based on the predicted results and acceptance criterion, a decision can be made if a particular App server can be moved or not. If it has to be moved, performance remediation measures have to be completed prior to the move.

The Table below depicts a real life situation for a corporation which went through a data center relocation project and conducted the *response time* study for 25 of its business-critical applications. The Apps marked green would meet user performance expectations. The Apps marked yellow were on the borderline of expectations and the one marked red would certainly not meet the user expectations. The Apps marked red should not be moved unless they can first be fixed to work better over the WAN.

Application	OK to move	Move with Caution	Do not move
ACJ	🟩		
Lab Instrument Tracking			🟥
Andromeda	🟩		
HRM	🟩		
RNN	🟩		
Alert 1	🟩		
LGS	🟩		
Millenium			🟥
Resource Reporting	🟩		
STLS - XX	🟩		
Static DB	🟩		
KLM	🟩		
Mercury	🟩		
SFF	🟩		
NNTS		🟨	
FDXX			🟥
PLOT 22		🟨	
XLF		🟨	
STDP	🟩		
MMGS	🟩		
Antmatter	🟩		
Element Management System	🟩		
NEAT			🟥
PHDS		🟨	
Many Item	🟩		
Extension Manager	🟩		

Table 1 Classification of Applications Considered for Data Center Relocation

The red-marked Apps in the Table are generally legacy, chatty applications that might have reached the end of their life cycle, in which case they can be replaced by next generation Apps providing equivalent functions. Converting these Apps into a Citrix-based application can often remediate the situation. In Citrix applications, only key-strokes/mouse clicks and text/graphics are transmitted over the WAN. The high chattiness will be confined to the data center where the Citrix server and the database reside.

For some well known applications, (e.g., CIFS file sharing) a new technology called WAN Optimization that has emerged in recent years can be applicable.

The key message one needs to take away here is to make the *response time* impact study an integral and unavoidable part of the data center relocation project.

DURING CLOUD MIGRATION

The trend of migrating to cloud-services is now one of the major undercurrents in the IT industry. Cloud offers the benefits of on-demand computing and storage services, improved costs, and flexibility needed in an ever changing business environment. Data security and end-user performance are the two primary issues for any company planning to migrate to the Cloud.

Cloud implies centralization of servers in a single data center (and in some cases a handful of data centers that the cloud providers offer as a choice). A *private Cloud,* in terms of performance will look like a case where multiple data centers of an enterprise are consolidated into a single enterprise data center. Hence all the issues we discussed in the previous section will come into force. If end-users are habituated to getting LAN-like performance, when the enterprise moves into a Cloud, there will be lots of unfulfilled expectations because of latency changes affecting chatty applications. Hence, a due diligence of performance investigation and remediation has to be conducted before move into a *private Cloud*. One benefit of the Cloud will be the availability of more flexible computing and memory resources, because of virtualization that typically accompanies any Cloud migration.

The above comments are still valid in the case of a company planning to buy *Infrastructure-as-a-service* or *Platform-as-a-service* type of Cloud services and deploy its own existing applications in the public Cloud, since the data center will now be remote to all the users. In the case of *Software-as-a-service (SaaS)* type of Cloud migration, the situation is slightly different. The onus of providing end-user *response time* SLAs will fall on the Cloud provider. In the SaaS case, the Cloud provider offers standard applications (for example, ERP or CRM) shared among many customers. Because of the wealth of resources available for Cloud providers, one can expect them to conduct thorough performance testing/tuning of the applications they offer on the Cloud to their customers.

A SaaS Cloud vendor may also offer enhanced performance as a premium service, and not offer any *response time* SLAs on the basic service.

CHAPTER 4

WHAT CAN WE DO ONCE THE APPLICATION IS ALREADY DEPLOYED?

In this chapter, we will examine various remediation techniques that can be used to improve *response time* for end-users. Implementing the best practices of APM during pre-deployment of Apps is like following a good diet and exercise regimen for good personal health. Performance issues will be minimal unless there are variations in the network/server infrastructure from what were assumed before deployment. IT infrastructures are not static, and the pattern of App usage can deviate widely from what was intended. Healthy people can fall sick and have to go to the doctor to get diagnosed and receive appropriate medication. APM companies, playing the role of a doctor for providing *response time* cures, have both straightforward and innovative techniques in their arsenal.

THE NETWORK ENVIRONMENT

It is instructive to understand the differences in the overall networking environment between a consumer/home set up and a corporate office set up. A typical consumer today has broadband (DSL or cable modem services or fiber services) at his/her home. The consumer might be able to get an almost *dedicated* downstream bandwidth of 512 kilobits/sec up to 10 Mbits/sec (or even more). The upstream is generally limited – from 256 kilobits/sec to a couple of Mbits/sec.

In the corporate environment we talk in terms of branches/ remote sites, regional offices, data centers, or headquarters. A branch may have 10-20 users with a shared connection of a high grade T1 line (1.544 Mbits/sec) or an even slower link such as 64 kilobits/sec. A regional office hosting hundreds to a few thousands of employees may share a DS3 (45 Mbits/sec). A data center hosting hundreds or even thousands of servers serving the entire corporation may have bandwidths in the OC3 (155 Mbits/sec) to OC12 (620 Mbits/sec). Note that corporate WAN links provide much higher grade connectivities in terms of availability/reliability as compared to consumer Internet connections.

Note that in the corporate environment, the bandwidths are *shared*. Although this implies that the bandwidth per employee is much less than that of a home user, it will be quite adequate because of *statistical multiplexing* – all users will not be consuming the bandwidth capacity at the same time. Even with 10 users, this phenomenon works well as each user accesses his application at different, small slices of time. For that small slice of time, a user would feel the availability of the entire bandwidth to him or her.

Such dedicated versus sharing of the bandwidth paths for a home user and a corporate user respectively, has some interesting implications for emerging technologies such as WAN Optimization that is discussed later.

There is another important category of network environment that can be hardly ignored - the Smartphone/Tablet-mobile network. This category, of course, applies not only to consumers but also to business users. Both of them use the currently available 3G or 4G mobile networks provided by service providers. The bandwidths available range from 512 Kbits/sec to a few Mbits/sec – with 4G this range is approaching 10 Mbits/sec to 18 Mbits/sec. The upstream bandwidth is typically from 128 kilobits/sec to a couple of Mbits/sec. With somewhat poor network characteristics in the areas of latency and packet loss, this category is the most challenging of the three types discussed so far.

One may also add a hybrid category to the network environment. This is where an employee is working virtual and using the home Internet access (sometimes business grade) to conduct office business. In this case the employee will be using some type of Virtual Private Network (VPN) to access their office applications. An employee could also be using a VPN with her Smartphone/Tablet via a mobile network, to access business applications.

THROW BANDWIDTH AT THE PROBLEM

Blaming the network and wanting to throw more bandwidth at it to solve *response* time problems has been the first instinct of many application owners (and often the perception from the end-user as well). The network is assumed to be guilty before any fair trial, and no wonder some APM vendors came up with T-shirts, with the slogan "It's not the Network" to be worn by the networking team members. Well, the network bandwidth is guilty some times and it can be detected by a trouble-shooting analysis of the App, using tools that can create pie charts like the one in Chapter 2.

A typical situation in which bandwidth is the culprit is one where an App which was mostly textual has been lately modified to include graphics and images. The client device will receive thousands of Kilobytes of data, instead of the few hundred Kilobytes earlier. The branch in which you work may have only a bandwidth of 64 kilobits/sec, which was OK when your App was textual. Now your response time may jump into double digits from a few seconds before. Increasing bandwidth from 64 Kbits/sec to a T1 (1.544 Mbits/sec) will very likely alleviate the *response time* issues in this case.

An indirect consequence may be when your App has not changed, but the App used by other users in the same branch was enhanced with images and graphics. Those users will be consuming the lion's share of the bandwidth and the resulting congestion on the link may slow down your App. In technical terms, the link may be operating at a higher *utilization* level (70% or more of the available bandwidth). Increasing bandwidth to the branch is the right action to take in this situation.

This situation could also be caused by employees using unauthorized applications (such as BitTorrent, video streaming) during the business hours. There are network monitoring tools that can detect use of these types of unauthorized applications by employees, and those Apps can be blocked by the network manager – thereby enhancing the performance level for all users

However, the problem may not be a scarcity of bandwidth. Many other factors could be causing or contributing to the slow response time. An application may have been changed with greatly increased chattiness. The application server may be overloaded or experiencing slow interactions with the database server. Moving the application into a Cloud may have significantly increased the latency.

The main message we want to give here is this: do not throw costly bandwidth blindly when there is a slow *response time* situation. First determine through a troubleshooting analysis whether a significant portion of the *response time* is coming from the bandwidth effect. If the results show that the bandwidth is the main culprit, you can consider the option of increasing it. Although the bandwidth costs in the wired world have come down significantly over the years, it still costs money to add bandwidth, especially the links that are corporate grade with high reliability.

Some comments on the Smartphone/mobile network usage and slow *response times* are appropriate here. With homes migrating to broadband speeds in the last several years, Websites have enriched their pages with graphics, images, video, and Java scripts. There has been some kind of a balance here for the user *response times*, because the increases in page sizes have been compensated with availability of higher bandwidths. With the rapid adoption of smartphones on mobile networks and the use bandwidths, an order of magnitude lower, this balance has been quite disturbed. A user will have a terrible experience accessing a website with rich multimedia pages, intended for a home broadband user.

Fortunately there is a catching up of the situation on two fronts. On one front the mobile service providers are migrating to 4G technologies with higher speeds, and on the other front, websites are being armed to serve web pages with contents optimized for receiving and viewing on Smartphones. In addition, the mobile browsers have also made provisions for recognizing a lower bandwidth environment.

In view of the above situation, one tends to jump to the conclusion that bandwidth is the culprit for slow mobile applications – this may not always be true. As the following pie chart indicates, in this particular example, client processing time on iPhone is the culprit for the login transaction. There is no substitute to conducting an unbiased troubleshooting analysis for arriving at the correct conclusion.

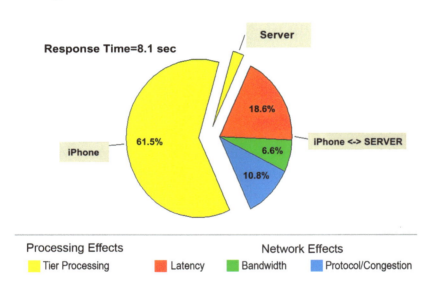

Figure 3 Response Time Pie chart for an iPhone App

MINIMIZING THE LATENCY-RELATED IMPACT

Let us say that you are in a great mood one Sunday afternoon for cooking your favorite dish. The recipe calls for ten ingredients. Fortunately all those ten ingredients are sitting in right your fridge. If you are a very organized person you will open the fridge door once, take all the ten ingredients, and lay them on the countertop before you start cooking. You are not a very organized person perhaps – you start cooking and reach for the ingredients one at a time, by opening the fridge door ten times during the cooking. Your dish turns out great nevertheless. Opening the fridge door ten times – that is how applications were coded some ten years ago. It did not matter much that you are a bit inefficient as you operated within your own 'kitchen', comparable to fetching everything you need instantaneously, on the LAN.

Imagine a situation where you do not have those ten ingredients in your kitchen. You have to drive to a grocery store two miles away and it takes ten minutes to make a roundtrip to the stores. Would you get the ingredients one at a time spending a total time of one hundred minutes? You may be a bit disorganized but not totally crazy. Well, many applications even today are written to make not just ten round trips but hundreds (in extreme cases, thousands) of roundtrips. The situation is truer with older generation applications, intended for use within a LAN, that are now deployed nationally or globally over a WAN. This characteristic of an application making a large number of roundtrips across the network is known as "chattiness". The one-way trip time of five minutes to your grocery stores is referred to as "latency".

In the above pie chart (Figure 3), the effect of latency on the *response time* amounts to 18.6% which is quite significant. Latency is the one-way transit time (at near the speed of light) traveling between the client and the server, through the various transmission paths (fiber, copper, and wireless). It is one-half of the "ping" delay or the roundtrip time, between the client machine and the server at the far end.

The range of latencies in real life is from a fraction of a milli-second to a few milliseconds on a LAN to 200+ milliseconds on a global WAN. By itself this number does not look daunting – it may rarely exceed 500 milliseconds in the worst case, to make one-round trip across the globe. But if your App is written in a way that it makes 100 roundtrips across the WAN (which is not that uncommon at all) to fetch the required data, the cumulative effect of latency would be 50 seconds. Your App *response time* will now be at least 50 seconds, not yet counting other effects such as bandwidth.

Let us discuss next how we can minimize the contribution to the *response time* of latency effects. Since the latency effect is directly proportional to the product of latency and application turns (round trips), both parameters need to be minimized to improve the *response time*.

Latency by itself cannot be reduced to below the speed-of-light propagation delay between any two geographical points across the network, at which the client device and the server are located. But steps can be taken to ensure that the latency is not too much higher than the propagation delay. Each router in the communication path contributes some (usually small) delay due to packet intake and processing, and these can add up. In a corporate WAN, the number of router hops can be minimized between the two end-points to reduce latency. If a service provider (e.g., offering MPLS) is used in the WAN, cer-tain SLAs can be demanded for latency between the two cit-ies. For example, AT&T provides an SLA of 50 milliseconds (one-way) across any two MPLS ports within the continental USA.

Latencies in the public Internet are higher and the variability is also high. If the client and the server are within the US, the range can be 10 ms to 80 ms. If the client is in the US and the server is in Europe/Asia-Pacific we can see latencies going up to 150 ms [4].

Latencies in the mobile networks are quite high and also have wide variability. It varies across the mobile carrier technologies (2.5G, 3G, or 4G) with better latencies in the newer generation networks. Latencies of a few hundred milliseconds are not that uncommon even on 3G networks.

The effects of latency can be mitigated to some extent by using Content Delivery Networks (CDNs). CDN providers have data centers all over the country and some worldwide. A customer's content is replicated across many data centers of the CDN provider, so that for any location there is a path of low latency to the content server. The web URL is automatically redirected to the nearest data center holding the content. CDN services are extensively used by media sites and movie streaming companies (e.g., Netflix). CDNs also serve the purpose of balancing the load among many servers during times of peak demand.

Application Chattiness As we observed earlier it is hard to have a prior knowledge of what range of latencies an application is going to encounter when it is deployed and widely used. A conservative approach would be to assume worst case latencies (even 100 ms one way) when designing/coding an application and keep chattiness extremely low.

Application chattiness can be measured in terms of the measure "Application Turns" (App turns). A turn means there is a change of direction in the application-level flow between the client and the server. Each time an application changes direction a delay, equal to one-way latency, occurs. The product of App Turns and latency gives a pretty good idea of the latency component of the delay in the response time. The App designer/coder must strive to keep App turns in low single digits as much as possible (ideal situation is one turn or one request-response pair).

App turns can be measured by tools (such as those from OPNET) by capturing a sample of the application transaction flow as it is being executed. High App turns in an application should be detected and fixed during the application development/testing stage itself. If we follow the best practice of using tools (that emulate or simulate the WAN) during the application development/testing stage, it is possible to design the application with very low App turns. Fortunately, there is a trend in this direction among the big application development organizations. But we can only hope that the best practice percolates into the smaller organizations soon.

There are lots of applications out there which are quite chatty, which may not be known to the App owner, and that are causing slow performance in the form of application chattiness. Once it is determined that chattiness is the root cause, there are a few options to make the App *response time* acceptable:

- Redesigning the web pages or re-coding the application to yield fewer turns. This option can be quite expensive for many corporate applications. Websites can be redesigned using recommendations from the **Yslow** tool.
- Using the services of a CDN provider
- If it is a corporate application, explore the possibilities of converting the application into a Citrix-based application.

- Again for a corporate application, for certain off-the-shelf applications, WAN Optimization solutions might work.

The CDN option was discussed before. The principles of the other options are discussed later in this chapter.

PROTOCOL EFFECTS

A predominant portion of applications use TCP/IP protocol. Voice-over-IP is one major application exception that uses the UDP protocol instead during the conversation phase. TCP protocol is known as a connection-oriented protocol, and it is used for reliable, sequenced, and error free transmission of data bytes between the client device and the server (and amongst servers). TCP was designed during the 1970's when networks were slow and error-prone. Some of the features designed for those conditions can become speed bumps in realizing the full potential of modern day networks running over extremely fast and reliable fiber-optic facilities. Of course, the mobile networks are not quite there yet and all TCP features still make lot of sense in that segment.

One common cause of slow App *response time* related to protocol, is a sub-optimal TCP Window setting. TCP protocol works by sending a sequence of data bytes from the sender and receiving acknowledgements of successful receipt of those data bytes from the receiver. The receiver (let us say the client laptop) signals the sender during the beginning of the session (let us say the server at the other end) that it can receive a certain maximum amount of data before sending an acknowledgement – this maximum size is known as the Window size. The Window mechanism prevents overflow of buffers at the receiver end.

Let us say that the bottleneck bandwidth between the laptop and the server is 2 Mbits/sec and the one-way latency between them is 100 ms. The Window setting on the older Microsoft OS laptops is generally 8 Kilobytes. This implies that once the server sends 8 Kilobytes of data to the laptop, it has to wait for the data to reach the laptop and for an acknowledgement to come back from the laptop, before sending any further data. This wait will be at least 200 ms (the round-trip delay). Hence the rate of data transfer on this link or the throughput cannot be more than 8 Kilobytes/0.2 sec or 40 Kilo**bytes** per sec, which is only 320 kilo**bits** per sec, and hence we are not able to fully utilize the 2 megabits per sec capacity of the link.

The correct Window setting in the above situation is 50 Kilobytes (which can be obtained by multiplying the bandwidth in bits/sec by the full round-trip delay and stating it in bytes (divide by 8)) – this number is called the Bandwidth-Delay Product). Most modern operating systems (including the Smartphones such as iPhones or Android phones) allow Window settings of 64 Kilobytes.

Maximum Window settings in excess of 64 Kilobytes may be required while operating on very high bandwidth and very high latency links. For example, if the available bandwidth on an international connection is OC3 (155 Mbits/sec) and the one-way latency is 150 ms, the Bandwidth-Delay Product is 5.81 Mbytes. In this case a Window setting of 4 Mbytes may be appropriate.

TCP allows Window settings above 64 Kilobytes by specifying a window scale factor in the protocol options field. This scale factor is the power of 2 which is multiplied by the base Window setting, to specify the real Window setting. In the above example, a scale factor of 6 on a 64 Kilobyte base Window will make the Window setting equal to 4 Mbytes (64K times 2 to the 6th power). A point to note is that keeping large Window sizes for all connections can waste memory if it is not really needed.

Another possible effect of TCP protocol on the App *response time* is the consequence of the use of the Nagel's algorithm feature. This feature is meant to minimize the sending of small sized messages to increase packet payload efficiency; but it can cause slowness because the algorithm waits for several small messages to appear before packaging them together for transmission. Nagel's algorithm can be turned off for a particular application or the application itself can be re-coded to avoid sending small messages.

Congestion

When network links in the application path are congested, meaning that more data is trying to enter the link than it has capacity for (similar to a traffic jam on a freeway), many things could happen that slows App *response times*. Packets could get queued up in the router buffers, waiting to be transmitted on the outgoing congested link. The cumulative queuing effects in the network will show up as increased App *response time* for the end-user. Also, packet losses can start occurring because of buffer overflows under heavy congestion conditions. Packet losses could also occur due to media collisions (e.g., in a LAN) or because of wireless signal interference.

TCP has inherent mechanisms for the retransmission of lost packets, so the data ultimately gets through, but at a slower pace. The TCP protocol also slows down the overall link packet transmission rate automatically when congestion and packet loss conditions are detected. During those times App *response times* will suffer. The protocol gradually reverts back to normal operation as congestion eases and packet losses cease to happen.

Quality of Service (QoS) mechanisms help packets belonging to mission critical and real-time applications get priority treatment in the network queues during congestion conditions. Packets are marked with class-of-service markers so that the network gives them the appropriate level of priority. For example, there are four classes currently used by AT&T – real-time, bursty high, bursty low, and best effort. Voice conversations and video conferencing are usually put in the real-time class, as they cannot be buffered. Mission critical applications should be put in the bursty high class to get the highest priority service for non-real-time traffic. For QoS mechanisms to work effectively, the QoS marking in each packet has to be preserved end-to-end, including the transit through the WAN provider or ISP.

SERVER-SIDE DELAYS

The next, but perhaps the most complex to understand part of the App *response time* delay, occurs on the server side. In the simplest case, we can have an App with only two tiers (a tier is a processing entity where the TCP protocol terminates or "closes"), the client machine and the App server, with the network in between. If the pie chart indicates server processing delay, the CPU capacity and/or the memory capacity of the server can be increased to *possibly* fix the problem, but there may be other causes of server delay, such as interactions with disk storage. If proper load testing under WAN conditions was done before the App deployment, this problem is unlikely to have occurred.

In most real-life scenarios applications are multi-tiered. Applications will typically involve a web server, an App server, and a database server. In corporate environments and web sites, applications with dozens of tiers may not be uncommon. Beyond identifying the total server-side component of the delay, we need to isolate the specific server or servers causing the delays.

For two-tier or multi-tier applications, server capacities may not be the cause of the slow *response time*. The various ways in which today's software components (e.g., Websphere, Java, and database) interact with each other could be causing slow *response time* issues. There are sophisticated tools to identify issues related to software components and the database components.

For web applications, the first tier between the client machine and the web server across the WAN often is the predominant cause of slow App response times. Identifying the issues with a tool like **Yslow** and following its recommendations can improve *response times* considerably.

For client-server applications, especially multi-tiered ones, the process of troubleshooting can become very challenging. When the application is already widely deployed and is in production mode, collecting the appropriate data at multiple tiers for analysis purposes is very difficult, since packet flows belonging to a single transaction often cannot be identified within the multitude of flows between servers in a production environment. Also, the system engineers managing the applications and servers are extremely leery of adding any new instrumentation in the application path or in the production servers because of the fear of disruption.

For off-the shelf applications such as Oracle, SAP, etc. there may be some prior knowledge of common performance issues in the software vendor's or user group's forums or FAQ database. For proprietary or home-grown applications, such an advantage would not exist.

The best way to manage application performance issues on the server/application side is to have already implemented sophisticated tools that can give visibility into server performance and understand application flows among different servers and databases. Such systems will not only monitor the App performance but will help predict and isolate performance issues, as they arise in the production environment. With those tools in place, the performance issues can be isolated to the server capacity/memory, application logic, and database queries.

Other than adding server capacity and/or memory, fixing application logic or changing the way database is queried can be an expensive proposition. When it comes to remediation of performance on the server side one need surely remember the old adage – *prevention is better than cure.*

CLIENT-SIDE DELAYS

As with servers, client machines are subject to processing delays that could slow down a particular application transaction. This effect is usually less than that on the server side, since the effect is confined to a single machine (such as a PC or laptop) that usually has fewer tasks to perform. Client machines have pre-configured software images and are well tuned for running specific business applications in a production environment. Sometimes, the client machine could have capacity issues or running an older operating system that contributes to slowness. The application could be requiring the client machine to do a large amount of processing (e.g., Java applets) during the course of the transaction. Often an upgrade in the client hardware or software will alleviate these problems.

Client-side delays are more common on consumer PCs/laptops. The user could knowingly or unknowingly be running many tasks in the background (including undetected malware) that impacts the performance of the application of immediate interest. Sometimes, well intended antivirus/spyware software could be consuming significant CPU/memory resources and slow down the user's intended application.

Client-side delays can be expected more often with Smartphone/Tablet Apps as those machines have relatively less powerful CPUs and less memory.

Converting an Application into a Citrix-based One

Let us say there is an application Z which runs very well when the client and the servers are located within the same LAN (developers love this – they don't have to be aware of issues like chattiness and amount of data transfers, but when deployed to a WAN, these issues will become significant). Now, instead of running the full client software in a remote PC, let us make the client part of the application run as an instance of an application on a larger server. Then we run a small application on a PC/ low-end desktop (thick-client) or a terminal with minimal intelligence (thin-client) and adequate memory. Now we can let a user access application Z over a WAN– all this application does is send input from the user (key-strokes and mouse movements) to the application Z via an intermediary program and receive/ display the results (data/graphics) on the user screen.

Now instead of running a single instance of application Z, we can, say, run 100 instances of Z in the server and each instance can correspond to a different user. The intermediary program can communicate with 100 users (or thin-clients) over the WAN. Because of limited amount of data (mostly textual and control information) and low chattiness, the WAN effects are minimal – the application can work well over a high latency and low bandwidth WAN.

The popular App "Go to my PC" advertized widely over the radio and elsewhere is a good example of this type of operation. Citrix is the name of the company that popularized this concept. Microsoft (its Terminal Server) and other companies have equivalent products. We will use the terminology "Citrifying" and "Citrification" to describe the process of converting a regular client-server application into one that is Citrix-based.

Although Citrification hides the backend inefficiencies and provides a good performance for the end-user, the overall experience is typically not the same as a well tuned client-server application running on a powerful desktop. But for workers in a large production environment where routine tasks have to be performed fast, Citrifying is a great technique. Actually the main goals of Citrification are simultaneous version control of an application to hundreds of users and minimizing calls to the help desk. The relatively inexpensive thin client terminals are another incentive if they have to be deployed in thousands of locations.

Citrifying an application that is well behaved on a LAN but ill-behaved on a WAN, because of chattiness or excessive data transfer, is always an option to be considered in many situations. For example, during a data center relocation a legacy application may not be friendly on the WAN and it may be hard/expensive to re-code the application - Citrifying may be the only option left in such cases. Another example of a case where Citrix can help is to extend an existing application to remote international branches that have low bandwidths and high latencies.

Multiple applications can be converted to Citrix and a menu of those applications can be made available on the user's screen. Citrix has gone a step further and virtualized entire desktops – multiple users can run their desktop operating systems and applications on a remote centralized server. Virtualized desktops are expected to simplify desktop provisioning and support.

One has to be aware that not all Citrix implementations have great App performance. Problems can arise on the front end because of high packet losses and excessive latencies. Also, at a remote site where bandwidth is shared among many users/applications, Citrix traffic has to be given a higher QoS ranking. Problems at the backend, such as insufficient memory and/or processing power on the servers hosting Citrix applications, could become a problem as more users are added. For example, slow printing is a common problem unless print settings are optimally configured.

WAN Optimization/WAN Acceleration

WAN Optimization, also known as WAN Acceleration (WANX), is one of the most innovative approaches to address App performance issues head on. The first generation of WANX devices was also referred to as Wide Area File Services (WAFS). WANX is most effective in enterprise environments where applications reside in a data center and are accessed by users in branches/remote sites dispersed geographically nationwide or worldwide. For certain applications and under certain conditions the performance improvements can be dramatic – the *response time* could improve 20 times from say 100 seconds to 5 seconds.

Do not expect WANX to improve performance if there are performance issues attributable to servers, databases, or application logic. Although WANX devices address chattiness issues of many commonly used off-the shelf applications, they do not address chattiness of home-grown or proprietary applications. But the WAN bandwidth savings they provide due to their compression techniques is in itself enough to justify their use in most enterprise networks.

WANX involves deploying devices in pairs – one in the data center and one in each branch/remote office. The one in the data center is a higher capacity unit and pairs with the smaller units in the branches. There are no standards defined (yet) in the WANX space, so the device pair has to belong to the same vendor. Although vendor implementations may vary, WANX devices work their magic in the following dimensions:

1. Compression – employs techniques for compressing the data that is leaving for the WAN and uncompressing it at the other end. Since less data is sent, compression makes the data transfer across the WAN faster and reduces utilization of the WAN links. Note that some data such as images and video may already be in the compressed form and cannot be compressed further.

2. Smart Caching – in any corporation there are repeated data patterns sent from the data center to a branch. For example multiple users may download the same word document during a day. The same document may be sent later in the day with minor modifications. There may be patterns like corporate logo for which there is no need to transmit the whole image every time. There are generally enough repetitive data patterns in day-to-day operations that can be detected, cached, and indexed in the WANX devices. When such a pattern is encountered, just the index data or pointers can be transmitted instead of the whole data. Caching works across all applications as it is done at the lower protocol levels.

Caching is very powerful as whole chunks of data now don't leave for the WAN journey at all and only small amounts of data carrying indexing information traverse the WAN. This means dramatically improved *response times* and reduction of traffic on the potentially congested WAN. Caching and compression together can cut WAN traffic very significantly, leaving the WAN links utilized at low levels. Enterprises can postpone adding expensive WAN capacities, and this is one of the key factors contributing to the ROI on WANX deployments.

3. TCP Optimization – The two WANX devices at the two ends of the WAN connection intercept TCP flow between the clients and the server and act as middlemen. Many TCP connections will be pre-set between the two WANX devices and will be ready to use instead of setting up a TCP connection on demand when a client is ready for a session. This saves some time on TCP connection setups and tear downs. The TCP connections between the WANX devices are optimized for taking full advantage of the available bandwidth and high quality (very low packet loss) of the transmission links. For example, the TCP Window sizes will be set to values higher than 64 Kbytes using Window scaling. Many of the TCP optimizations are vendor specific. All these optimizations are transparent to the client-server communication, but the end result is the perceived increased throughput and faster *response time* for the user.

4. Reducing Chattiness – The above techniques will be applicable to all the applications running over the WAN connection. WANXs also perform some application

specific improvements. In those cases the WANX device at the branch acts as a proxy to the server, and the WANX device at the data center acts as proxy to the client. The WANX devices are good at removing chattiness from many standard applications such as Microsoft CIFS (file sharing), MS-SQL etc. The leading WANX vendors keep adding new applications to their list of optimization capabilities.

The WANX devices can also provide the local File services and eliminate the need for File servers at the branches, saving a lot of maintenance costs.

Dual WANX devices (or N+1 redundancy) can be configured to provide high availability at the data center. WANX devices are definitely helping companies to alleviate *response time* issues and save WAN costs. They have become a mainstream product in the enterprise network architecture and are here to stay.

Upcoming Server-side Improvements

There are companies constantly innovating to improve App performance from the server side. Most of them pertain to improving performance of web-based applications. A company called Aptimize (now acquired by Riverbed Technologies) has a software product that runs in the web server and does some page optimizations during the run time before a page is fetched into the WAN. The optimization comes from implementing, on the fly, some of the recommendations from **Yslow** – examples include reducing the complexities of having too many objects, dealing with bigger page sizes, exploiting repeat visits of the websites, and creatively handling browser diversity.

There are other companies such as Zeus (again acquired by Riverbed Technologies) that have virtualized the traditional hardware-based load balancer and added performance improving functionalities. The techniques they employ include offloading encryption/compression tasks from the web server, dynamic caching, and directing web requests to the data center with the lowest latency. Such products are targeted at e-commerce sites and help maximize their revenues by intelligently handling peak-time loads.

LOAD TESTING

Load testing practice has been entrenched in the IT industry for more than a decade. Load testing reveals the performance of the server and the system under an expected load of concurrent virtual users. The load testing software can run scripts of the selected transactions of an application and ramp up the load on the system gradually. In addition to the *response time* behavior of the servers, a load test can reveal other flaws in the application such as those related to security.

One main issue with the load testing process is that it is conducted on the LAN most of the time. Fortunately there is a recent trend to integrate WAN emulation into the load testing software and this is strongly recommended. Some vendors also test the servers from "outside-in" by involving the real WAN itself or the Internet.

The principles of load testing (i.e., using automated synthetic transactions) are also used in the production environment to gauge the *response times* of transactions, by executing the synthetic transactions at regular intervals along with the real users.

CHAPTER 5

TOOLS FOR APPLICATION PERFORMANCE MANAGEMENT

Measurement and analysis tools are a very important and key component of any APM strategy. If you cannot measure something accurately, you cannot control and manage it. Since APM issues span multiple disciplines such as software, networking, and server engineering, the tools that have been in place tend to be siloed within the respective organizations. Just like the five blind-men in the fable feeling different parts of an elephant and coming to different conclusions, each such tool will tell only part of the story. An engineer who just looks at the tool which monitors server CPU, memory, and disk I/O utilization may come to the wrong conclusion that all applications running on that server are providing good *response times* to the end-users.

In this chapter, we will review the concepts and approaches behind the tools that span across multiple domains and strive to provide insights and metrics that are targeted towards the real end-user *response times*. Because of our extensive experience with one tool vendor, OPNET Technologies, we have gone into detail, describing the salient features of OPNET's family of tools. There are other equivalent tools to OPNET that customers use and we will mention them towards the end of the chapter.

End-user application *response time*, although extremely easy to understand, is very difficult to measure in an automated way. With the exception of web page download time measurements incorporated into a web browser, there are few cases of non-web applications where true *response time* measurements are generated as a part of the application itself. Another exception is when a user performs a search on Google, and the time it took to perform the search is also displayed along with the results. If we can do the same for every application and harness the measurements, we would have very few APM issues! Unfortunately we are still quite far away from that goal.

TRANSACTION FOCUSED TOOLS

Let us start with the tool that generated the pie chart (Figures 2 and 3) – the name of the tool is *AppTransaction Xpert* from OPNET Technologies. As the name implies the tool focuses on analyzing individual transactions within an application. A transaction is defined as any operation that involves a user-initiated action (such as clicking on a link or hitting a return button) on the client machine and getting a response from the application. Examples of transactions are login, opening an email attachment, or clicking on a web URL. The OPNET tool uses the pattern of packet flows to break down the sources of the delays within the transaction, thus giving us a result such as those pie charts. Another company that makes a similar tool is Compuware.

The input to such a tool comprises an actual packet trace obtained by a Sniffer or Wireshark or a software agent in the application path that captures a copy of the packet flow – typically obtained at the client end or the server end or both. With some additional inputs such as the bottleneck bandwidth in the transaction path and the latency between the client and the server, the tool performs packet flow analytics and will be able to render a breakdown of the *response time* into different components – client, bandwidth, latency/chattiness, server, protocol, and congestion. The tool also provides other meaningful metrics such as the amount of data transferred, application chattiness, packet losses, throughput over the transaction period, and TCP connection resets. The tool has a rich set of features including a diagnostics summary and even generating a word report.

*OPNET's **AppTransaction Xpert*** tool also can perform *response time* predictions for different network (such as bandwidth and latency) and application (like chattiness) scenarios. Prediction capabilities are very useful for testing application readiness before a new deployment or before changing network architectures such as during a data center relocation or incorporating WAN Optimization. The tool has advanced capabilities like discrete event simulation, where an entire enterprise network with servers/clients could be modeled and application scenarios with different patterns of usage at different client sites can be studied for *response time* and other useful metrics.

The tool can also be deployed for troubleshooting in an ongoing monitoring environment. In this case software agents that perform continuous capture can be deployed on all user desktops/laptops and users can initiate a trouble ticket to a centralized server whenever they encounter a slow transaction. The server will send an alert to a human analyst who can then retrieve the transaction trace for the "problem period" and troubleshoot the cause of slow *response time*.

In summary, OPNET's ***AppTransaction Xpert*** tool is a very useful tool for pre-deployment planning and post-deployment troubleshooting/monitoring.

MACRO LEVEL FLOW ANALYSIS TOOLS

Whereas the tool we talked about above is like a microscope (it focuses deeply on a single transaction at a time), we have another complementary type of tool which is telescopic in characteristics – it collects, observers, and analyzes all the traffic flowing at certain vantage points in the network, to determine how each of the applications on that path are performing. Conceptually the tool is a "super sniffer" capturing all packet data (either the full packets, or only the TCP/UDP headers, or just rolled-up information from the headers) flowing through that point to a large capacity disk (typically 300 GBytes to a several TerraBytes). Once we have the packet headers and their arrival times recorded, a lot of very useful analysis can be carried out by the analytics engine that yields insights on App performance as well as useful traffic flow statistics between various end points.

One such tool is again from OPNET Technologies and is called *AppResponse Xpert.* There are similar tools from Riverbed Technologies in their **Cascade** family of tools. These tools are able to look at each TCP session between a client and a server in its entirety – from the TCP connection set up to a TCP connection tear-down across all clients in an enterprise. Every application data request/response between a client and a server is comprised of one or several TCP connections. By analyzing the TCP packet flow the tool will be able to provide important metrics over any chosen period and chosen set of sites/users/ applications such as:

- TCP Connect time (the time for the 3-way handshake)
- Server response time
- Data Transfer time
- Chattiness level or TCP-level Turns
- Round Trip Times between the client and the server
- Number of TCP connections
- TCP Connection Resets

Based on the above TCP flow level metrics, the tool is able to give a *sense* of the end-user *response time*. This *response time* is not a true transaction response time (from a user experience point of view, as is done in *AppTransaction Xpert*) but an atomic response time for each request/response pair within a user transaction. Since the tool is not aware of the boundaries of a user transaction (as when a user clicks a link and gets the entire web page downloaded) it cannot determine the true transactional application response time. Nevertheless the *response time* esti-mated by the tool is of great value on a relative basis. For exam-ple if the user *response time* shown by the tool doubles from week to week, it definitely means the transactional user *response time* is deteriorating as well. Also a slow server response time is an indicator of a busy server, which is very useful to know.

For websites, the tool will be able to provide page download times of various URLs and these represent the true end-user *response times*.

The *AppResponse Xpert tool* has the nice feature of defin-ing business groups based on IP addresses. These groups can be formed in many ways such as physical locations (e.g., remote sites) and functional groups (e.g., SAP). In addition to the TCP metrics that were mentioned, the following metrics can be reviewed between any defined groups and drilled down to indi-vidual conversation pairs:

- Throughput
- Packet loss
- Top N applications
- Percentage of bandwidth consumed by each application

The *AppResponse Xpert tool* is also a great tool for estimat-ing bandwidth changes needed at the branches and data center during a data center relocation/consolidation project. OPNET has done a nice job of integrating the two tools – one can capture packet data between a user and the server using the *AppResponse Xpert* tool and launch the *AppTransaction Xpert* tool to con-duct an application transaction analysis. One can also initiate and control packet captures on *AppResponse Xpert* from an *AppTransaction Xpert* console.

Server/Application side Tools

If there are server delays in the end-user *response times*, the tools discussed in the previous two sections can help in identifying and allocating that component to one or more servers. But we would not know if the server delay is because of CPU, memory, disk I/O, application components, database queries or something else. There are software tools to help drill down into the sources of delay in the server/application/database. These tools require that small-footprint software agents run in the servers, to collect the needed data from the server OS, application, and database components. They then feed collected measurements into a central server with a software engine that can perform various analytics and correlations to help isolate the causes of slow performance.

Again OPNET has an excellent tool called *AppInternals Xpert* for server/application side application performance analysis. We are directly quoting here from OPNET's website [5]:

"*AppInternals Xpert* delves into the complex software frameworks and operating systems of modern servers to extract vast amounts of performance and forensic data to support all aspects of APM from the server perspective. *AppInternals Xpert* can provide analysis for any type of application, but excels, in particular, in Java and .NET environments. It continuously monitors thousands of system and application metrics within each server, across all application tiers, and automatically detects and ranks performance and behavior anomalies.

"AppInternals Xpert uses patented technology to automatically provide deep instrumentation in application code with very low overhead. Its patented correlation technology automatically reveals relationships among metrics, highlighting the corresponding causal connections between components, resources, and behavior to perform root cause analysis. *AppInternals Xpert* also utilizes advanced, low-overhead, continuous tracing techniques to provide deep visibility into application code as it executes. It can assemble a complete picture of a transaction's path across tiers, for near real-time and historical analysis."

AppInternals Xpert can be used to:

- Monitor applications at the component level to proactively detect performance problems.
- Troubleshoot website errors and overall slowness.
- Troubleshoot intermittent performance problems.
- Troubleshoot packaged applications such as SharePoint, PeopleSoft, and Documentum, by bringing evidence of performance issues to vendors and implementers.
- Continuously monitor applications to detect memory leaks.
- Analyze applications prior to deployment, identifying slow Java or .NET methods and other resource bottlenecks that can impact performance in production.
- Establish a cohesive view of the application that spans multiple silos with cross-domain triage.

For database performance, OPNET offers a tool called *AppSQL Xpert* that provides deep analysis of database performance, while offering an agent-less approach that imposes zero overhead on database operation.

OPNET has done a very fine job of integrating its various APM tools by providing the capability to launch them from an *AppResponse Xpert* dashboard.

OTHER IMPORTANT TOOLS

We have stressed throughout this book the importance of incorporating WAN factors into any performance analysis/ testing effort. While OPNET tools use simulation approaches to model a WAN, Shunra Software Ltd. [6] has an appliance type of product that can perform WAN emulation by emulating WAN behavior in terms of bandwidth, latency, packet loss, and jitter. Thus, the tool allows the actual application and its real clients/servers to run over an expected WAN environment, allowing users to experience the actual impact of a WAN environment in real time. The Shunra tool is very handy in a development environment where the developers can incorporate a "WAN" culture into all their testing steps. Shunra has also partnered with HP to integrate WAN emulation into the HP Load Runner's tool set.

Gartner has announced their 2011 Magic Quadrant of Application Performance Monitoring that includes companies that are classified as Leaders, Challengers, Visionaries, and Niche players. The companies listed in the Leaders quadrant are: IBM, CA, Compuware, Quest Software, HP, OPNET, and Optier. For more details the reader is referred to the complete report [7]. One interesting company in the Visionaries quadrant is Knoa Software [8]. Knoa has an innovative way of measuring true end-user transaction *response times* by interfacing at the graphical user interface and operating system level. But the software does not work across all applications – nevertheless Knoa's software is very helpful in monitoring specific off-the-shelf mission critical applications such as those from leading CRM and ERP vendors.

Notice that Garter distinguishes between Monitoring and Management. Monitoring is concerned with ongoing efforts to preserve, report, and troubleshoot performance of applications that are already deployed. We have taken the Application Performance *Management* perspective throughout this book which also encompasses Application Performance Engineering and pre-deployment planning/testing.

CHAPTER 6

PERFORMANCE MANAGEMENT – OTHER SCENARIOS

There are a few topics related to Application Performance Management that we have not discussed in this book and this chapter offers some brief views on those topics.

NON-END-USER APPLICATION PERFORMANCE (M2M)

Throughout this book, we focused totally on end-user performance and *response time*, examined the causes of slow performance, and discussed various remediation techniques to improve performance. If there is no end-user sitting in front of a client machine we would have a scenario where one machine is interacting with the other machine, the server, at the far end. The distinction between a server machine and a client machine is mere semantics – the client is the machine that initiates the TCP communication and the other one becomes the server.

One important example of non-end-user oriented server to server communication is the one that takes place during data backup/replication between a main data center and a backup or Disaster Recovery (DR) data center. It is critical that the replication operation is done in almost real-time and backup is completed within the allotted window of operation. Both operations are affected by the same network impairments and application chattiness issues that we discussed in the context of end-user *response time*. Many of the techniques used to improve end-user *response time* have found applicability in the replication/backup operations. WAN Optimization products from vendors such as Riverbed and Silver Peak are now routinely used in data centers to improve replication/backup performance and meet Recovery Point and Recovery Time Objectives (RPOs and RTO's).

Internet technology is making inroads into the world of home appliances (refrigerator, washing machines, and smart thermostats) and industrial devices (surveillance cameras, wireless health monitoring, industrial controllers). When two machines communicate with each there will be situations where a specific *response time* objective has to be built into the design of the system. As the two machines communicate with each other using TCP/IP over the Internet or private networks or wireless/mobile networks, we will encounter similar performance issues as with the challenges of delivering a good *response time* to an end-user – the requirements are likely to be even more stringent than a two-second *response time*. Hopefully many of the APM techniques of today can be applied to solve *response time* problems in the burgeoning field of machine-to-machine (M2M) communication.

VOICE-OVER-IP

To begin with, we have so far not mentioned Voice at all, specifically Voice-over-IP or VOIP – Voice is definitely a mission critical application for an enterprise. Fortunately, Voice is a well known user application that has existed for over one hundred years and its performance characteristics are very well understood. Voice also has a traditional well accepted metric, Mean Opinion Score (MOS) for judging voice quality.

Many of the impairments that affect a data application apply to VOIP as well – inadequate bandwidth, latency, and packet loss. In addition, the variability of latency, known as jitter, is a very important parameter since it affects voice quality – jitter is less of a concern for a data application. Another important distinction is that VOIP uses UDP protocol for packet transfer after a call is set up. UDP is a "connectionless" protocol which does not have built-in error detection and packet retransmission mechanisms, as TCP does, but it delivers an uninterrupted stream of data that is needed for voice.

Companies planning to deploy VOIP in their enterprise network are recommended to test their network for VOIP readiness. If remediation is done to correct any shortcomings coming out of a VOIP readiness test and then the VOIP technology is deployed, one can expect minimal issues. One very important task is to ensure that Voice traffic is set to receive the highest

QoS (the real-time class) and that enough bandwidth is allocated for that class (especially at the remote sites).

If an enterprise uses an advanced WAN technology such as MPLS with a real-time QoS class from a reputed service provider, one can expect very few problems with the VOIP quality. There could still be some performance issues for a mid-sized company using internet-based VPNs for its international sites.

Another piece of good news for enterprise VOIP is that the equipment providers (at least the big ones such as Cisco and Avaya) provide the needed tools and support for monitoring the VOIP quality.

VOIP quality has greatly improved among internet-based VOIP service providers (such as Vonage, Comcast) and there is generally medium to high user satisfaction among users (given the huge economic benefits of VOIP). There are still pockets of VOIP scenarios where the quality is still considered poor – for example, VOIP with a Smartphone over a mobile network.

Real-time video conferencing is also becoming popular over WAN environments, and interactive video will experience the same kind of issues as VOIP, although at higher bandwidths.

VIDEO/AUDIO STREAMING

With the popularity of online video streaming from companies such as Netflix and Audio streaming from Pandora, it is worthwhile to understand these services with reference to performance issues. The streaming services have to encounter the same good old network impairments – bandwidth limitation, latency, jitter, packet loss, and out of sequence packets. But as we have experienced both video and audio can be rendered perfectly over the Internet and even mobile networks (for audio only). The trick here is to use TCP/IP protocol instead of UDP (TCP delivers error free communication whereas UDP does not) and introduce a small amount of delay (typically a minute or two) to facilitate buffering. This is possible since streaming is one-way from a user point of view, rather than interactive, and some one-time initial delay is tolerable.

Once there are enough packets in the buffer to play the audio or video for a minute or two, the remaining packets can be transferred reliably in the background while the video and audio program starts playing for the user. In the case of an online movie, the reliable packet flow continues until the whole movie is delivered in the background. In the case of an ongoing video/audio streaming the delivery is continuous to the user. The users get an experience of high quality audio/video streaming after the initial delay. If the network quality is not that great the initial delay can be high and also there could be occasional hiccups during the streaming.

CHAPTER 7

CONCLUDING THOUGHTS

One can only control and improve those parameters that can be measured accurately. End-user *response time* is such an easy concept that everybody can feel it, understand it, and complain about it. But if you ask somebody if they are getting a six-second or a twelve-second *response time* in the application they are complaining about, it is unlikely they will be able to give a good answer. What is more interesting is none of the tool vendors have an elegant, non-intrusive, and automated way of measuring and recording end-user *response time* across all applications and user platforms. There is perhaps a need for some innovation here– didn't Wilbur Scoville invent a creative way to measure the piquancy of chili peppers?

One of the challenges of measuring *response time* is the inability to automatically recognize the boundaries of an application transaction (the beginning and end) – only the end-user knows it and can feel the wait time. Machines currently cannot pick out all the user actions and corresponding responses that humans can experience when interacting with the wide variety of applications and platforms available today. Manual measurements taken in concert with an end-user work well but they have the disadvantage of being spot measurements at that time, which may miss the poor response time that occurs intermittently In a production environment of any corporation there is an understandable extreme reluctance to interfere with a line worker's daily routine. The complaints to the help desk tend to be anecdotal with less specificity as regards to the time and what particular transaction was slow.

Given that this situation is not likely to change anytime soon, an enterprise is well advised to follow the age old adage we quoted earlier– *prevention is better than cure*. What this means is:

- The application developers need to do a thorough job of pre-deployment performance testing of a single-user case with full awareness of the network environment over which the application will be deployed – at least the latency and bandwidth. The application chattiness has to be kept very low – preferably in the low single digits per transaction. The multi-user load-testing [1] has to be conducted in an environment that is as close to the production one as possible. It is the earlier the better that the application and network teams begin to collaborate before every application roll-out. This early planning ensures that network infrastructure can provide the required bandwidth and QoS features needed.

- The network infrastructure team has to be cognizant of the fact that even small changes to the network, not well planned, could have impact on performance of business critical applications. Major changes such as router upgrades, introduction of WAN Optimization, adding voice-over-IP, data center relocations, and cloud-migration have to be planned carefully in a pro-active mode of communication with application owners and their teams.

It is also our experience that in large companies, even some best-in-class, there is a tendency between the application and network teams to indulge in blame games. One way to foster better collaboration between the two teams is to create an office of the Chief Performance Officer (CPO) who has the responsibility for the overall application performance for the whole company. The CPO (reporting to the CIO) can help in sharing the best practices, processes, and tools needed to achieve superior application performance among multiple application owners across different business units. The CPO would also fulfill the important need of setting up and monitoring performance SLAs for the Cloud vendors.

The increasing adoption of Cloud computing among many small/mid-sized companies and the eventual spread of the paradigm to large corporations presents both challenges and opportunities. The centralization of the servers means there are no "LAN applications" any more. All application access is via WAN/Internet, which means exposure to variable and longer latencies and reduced bandwidth. As discussed throughout this book, these consequences obviously cannot be good for end-user *response times*. Trouble-shooting becomes more complex as the servers/applications are in the Cloud vendor's data center. One benefit that can come out of Software-as-a-service Cloud model is the emergence of more standardized, cookie-cutter type of applications. Because of the scale of usage, the Cloud vendor is likely to invest heavily in pre-deployment testing of these applications; the vendor may even be able to offer performance SLAs as a value added service.

Another challenge in the APM area is the ongoing adoption of smartphone/Tablet applications in the corporate environment (which is somewhat trailing behind the consumer adoption). Those mobile devices while using Wi-Fi can be expected to have similar levels of App performance issues as PCs or laptops. The challenges arise when users come to expect similar performance on public mobile networks. Although the download speeds are seeing great improvements with 4G technology, longer latencies and higher packet losses can become formidable issues for providing great user experience.

Motivated readers interested in understanding APM issues in more detail are encouraged to browse through the case studies [9] provided in the referenced website. The abstracts of those case studies are included in the Appendix.

APPENDIX

ABSTRACTS OF CUSTOMER CASE STUDIES

CASE STUDY #7

PERFORMANCE ASSESSMENT DURING CLOUD MIGRATION

A leading bio-tech company wanted to consolidate their five data centers into a private Cloud architecture. The two major concerns were the post-migration performance of their fifty business critical applications and the bandwidth requirements at the current/new Cloud data centers.

A two-track assessment project was conducted - one focusing on response time analysis and the other on bandwidth estimation, both using OPNET tools. Using ACE Analyst (*AppTransaction Xpert*), the project identified which critical applications can be moved without much degradation and made mitigating recommendations for the ones that had issues. By leveraging the business group traffic flow feature in ACE Live (*AppResponse Xpert*) and manipulating server traffic flows, bandwidth estimations were provided.

The case study discusses the methodology, highlights the technical/project issues encountered, and how those were overcome.

Link:

http://www.apseratech.com/cloud-mobile.php

CASE STUDY #2

iPhone Performance Analysis

The iPhone has become the Smartphone of choice among many consumers and business users. The requirement of a fast response time applies equally well to a Smartphone application as to a PC-based application in a wired network. There is the usual finger-pointing game because application response times are relatively slower in a mobile environment.

This briefing brings the valuable OPNET ACE analysis (using *App Transaction Xpert*) to the study of the common applications used on an iPhone. By creatively capturing traffic on both Wifi and 3G networks and conducting an ACE analysis, the response times are broken down into client, network, and the server components. The throughputs obtainable on an iPhone over 3G and Wifi are observed.

The study helps to dispel some popular myths in the mobile arena and help increase awareness of performance issues among users and iPhone application developers.

Link:

http://www.apseratech.com/iphone.php

CASE STUDY #3

APPLICATION PERFORMANCE BENCHMARKING DURING SERVER RELOCATION

As a part of its Disaster Recovery strategy, a major regional bank was in the process of moving all servers away from the hurricane-prone area. This server relocation was changing bandwidths and latencies between the end-user machines and the servers/databases and might have resulted in changes to end-user performance, especially for interactive type of transactions.

The bank used OPNET *AppTransaction Xpert* to help track and manage the performance changes by benchmarking response times for representative applications at representative sites before the server relocation. This project briefing describes the steps in the benchmarking effort and how the data was used to mitigate any possible performance issues post-relocation.

Link:

http://www.apseratech.com/case_studies_ppt.php

CASE STUDY #4

ASSORTED SME TRAFFIC BASELINING CASE STUDIES

Many Small/Medium Enterprises (SMEs) do not implement instrumentation for ongoing monitoring of the WAN links either because of the cost of the devices or the need to dedicate staff. There are always events such as data center relocation, sales-day events, bandwidth abuse, and new traffic patterns that require them to perform at least a one-time traffic baselining to address the immediate business need.

This technical briefing describes several case studies of Traffic Baselining using OPNET ACE Live/*AppResponse Xpert* tool (formerly Network Physics). ACE Live's easy to install and remote-access features, and its rich set of reports from circuit level to TCP level to application level made it an ideal choice for one-time baselining. This briefing demonstrates how each customer had a different business motive for performing the Traffic

Baselining and how all of them benefited from the analysis/ interpretation of the various charts mined from the ACE Live device.

Link:

http://www.apseratech.com/case_studies_ppt.php

CASE STUDY #5

TRAFFIC BASELINING CASE STUDY

The customer wanted a traffic baseline and analysis of their MPLS-based WAN. The purpose of the baselining/analysis was to validate the customer's proposed bandwidth upgrades of their data center and some remote links. The customer was also embarking on the deployment of a new version of SAP and had some concerns about additional bandwidth requirements.

A traffic study was conducted by deploying OPNET ACE Live (*AppResponse Xpert*) in the data center and collecting data for a week. By setting up appropriate business groups and analyzing the various traffic flows, a comprehensive view of the current status of their network and the pattern of usage by different applications was provided. The traffic study helped the customer to make informed decisions regarding the bandwidth upgrades.

Link:

http://www.apseratech.com/traffic_baseline_casestudies.php

CASE STUDY #6

PERFORMANCE AND CAPACITY PLANNING FOR NEW APPLICATION ROLL-OUT

The customer, a major retail store in healthcare industry was planning to roll out many new applications over its network of several thousand retail stores.

They wanted to ensure adequate network capacity is available for the new applications as well as existing applications. An optimal trade-off between bandwidth at the retail stores and application response time was important because of the huge number of retail stores and associated WAN costs.

Using OPNET *AppTransaction Xpert*, the first application suite was baselined and an analysis/simulation was performed for the various transactions of the application. It was determined that bandwidth and background utilization rather latencies were the major factors affecting the performance. Guidelines were provided for appropriate link sizing in order to meet the desired performance goals.

Link:

http://www.apseratech.com/performance_capacity_planning.php

REFERENCES

1. Scott Barber and Colin Mason, Web Load Testing for Dummies, eBook, Compuware Corporation, 2011
2. Steve Souders, High Performance Web Sites: Essential Knowledge for Frontend Engineers, O'Reilly, 2007
3. Steve Souders, Even Faster Web sites: Performance Best Practices for Web Developers, O'Reilly, 2009
4. http://www.caida.org/research/performance/rtt/walrus0202/
5. OPNET Technologies Inc., web site, www.opnet.com
6. Shunra Software Ltd., website, www.shunra.com
7. Magic Quadrant for Application Performance Monitoring, 19 September 2011, Will Cappelli and Jonah Kowall, Gartner Research Note G00215740
8. Knoa Software Inc., website, www.knoa.com
9. Apsera Tech Inc., website, www.apseratech.com

ABOUT THE AUTHORS

Dr. Sampath Prakash - President and CEO of Apsera Tech Inc.

Sampath Prakash founded Apsera Tech Inc, a company focused on providing application performance and WAN Acceleration consulting, in January 2005. His past work experience has been with various organizations within AT&T stretching for over nineteen years. Prior to Apsera Tech, Prakash was a practice director at AT&T Professional Services. He created various practices that helped AT&T's business customers implement best practices in networking strategy, architecture, design, performance, security, reliability, management and processes. Before his professional services tenure, he spent eleven years at Bell Laboratories working on architectural and performance aspects of AT&T's Global Network.

Prakash has a Ph.D. in Electrical Engineering from IIT, Madras and holds industry certifications such as PMP, CISSP, OPNET, and Six-Sigma.

John Sikora - Chief Technology Consultant of Apsera Tech Inc

John Sikora joined Apsera Tech Inc in January, 2009, and has focused on application performance, traffic analysis and WAN Acceleration consulting. His past work experience has been with various technical organizations within AT&T for over thirty-five years. Prior to Apsera Tech, John was a senior technical consultant at AT&T Professional Services. He worked with many business customers to provide consulting in application performance, application infrastructure reliability, performance management, network management, and WAN acceleration. Before his professional services tenure, he spent twenty-five years as a technical manager at Bell/AT&T Laboratories working on data communications, data networking, and network architecture.

John has a Masters Degree in Electrical Engineering from the University of Wisconsin, and was a Wisconsin State Fellow. He is the holder of three patents in the area of data networking.

INDEX